Graceful swags of garland add a dramatic touch to a room. Whether the garlands are made from fresh, preserved, or artificial greens, they can be embellished for an impressive statement.

Fresh garlands are quick and easy to make, and handmade fresh garlands have a fuller shape than purchased ones. When making your own, mix different varieties of greens for added color and texture. Fresh cuttings can often be purchased by weight from nurseries. Cedar greens work especially well for indoor use; they do not shed, and they keep their color longer than most varieties.

For the realistic look of fresh garlands, use dried or preserved greens. They last longer than fresh garlands and can be used for more than one season. For a garland that can be used year after year, use artificial greens. To add the fragrance of evergreen, embellish the garland with scented pinecones or tuck in a few sprigs of fresh greens.

HOW TO MAKE A FRESH GARLAND

MATERIALS

- Fresh greens.
- Lightweight rope or twine.
- 22-gauge paddle floral wire or chenille stems.
- Pruning shears.
- Wire cutter.

1 Tie rope to solid overhead object, such as ceiling-mounted plant hook. Cut fresh greens into sprigs. Wire three sprigs to rope, with tips facing up, placing two in front and one in back; wrap wire at the base of the sprigs.

2 Continue wiring greens around rope, overlapping them to conceal the wire. At desired length, wire full tips of greens to bottom of garland, concealing ends of sprigs.

3 Cut the wire and rope at ends of garland; knot ends, forming loops for hanging, if desired.

MORE IDEAS FOR GARLANDS

Garland *is used traditionally to dress the mantel. To secure the garland without nailing into the mantel itself, cut a 1 × 1 board the length of the mantel. Stain or paint the board to match the mantel, and pound nails into the board for securing the garland.*

Swag *is draped high above a fireplace, and sprays are displayed on each side. To make a pair of sprays from an artificial garland, cut a 9-foot (2.75 meter) garland in half. Fold each piece in half, creating two sprays, and embellish them as desired.*

Safety note: *Do not leave any open flame, including candles, unattended. For fireplaces, always use a fire screen. (Screen was removed for photo effect.)*

Bow-shaped garland is hung over the fireplace instead of a wreath. Tie a wide ribbon to the ends of the garland, and hang the garland from the ribbon.

Fresh garland is used to decorate a bannister. To protect wood surfaces, use chenille stems instead of wire when making the garland.

HOLIDAY BOWS

Lavish bows and streamers are often a finishing touch for holiday decorations. Use ribbons in the traditional red and green, or in colors to match the decor of the room.

The key to achieving a luxurious look is to be generous with the ribbon. The size of the bow should be in proportion to the project being embellished. For example, large garlands require large, full bows with long streamers; for large bows, use wide, stiff ribbons.

Craft ribbon is available in several fabric types, including taffeta, moiré, satin, and velvet. French ribbon, sometimes called wired ribbon, makes beautiful bows. The fine wires that run along the edges of the ribbon can be bent into curves and folds, giving bows an old-world look that is distinctly elegant. For a more homespun or country look, bows can be made from paper twist.

Two styles of bows are so versatile that they meet most holiday decorating needs: the cluster bow and the traditional bow.

The cluster bow can easily be made in any size. To estimate the ribbon yardage, multiply the desired diameter of the bow times the number of loops desired. Add 6" (15 cm) to this measurement for the center loop plus the desired amount for tails and extra streamers.

The traditional bow is commonly used for wreaths, but also works well for elegant packages. For a 7" to 8" (18 to 20.5 cm) bow, you will need 2½ yd.

Plaid taffeta ribbon *is used for the large cluster bow on this spray of greens. For added embellishment, pinecones surround the bow.*

Two layers of French ribbon, treated as one, are used for the cluster bow on this tiered plate stand.

Sheer metallic ribbon in cluster bows adorns a pair of candlesticks.

Taffeta French ribbon, tied into a traditional bow, embellishes this Christmas package.

Paper twist is used instead of ribbon for the traditional bow on a fruit basket.

French ribbon makes the cluster bow for this ivy plant. For an ivy wreath, secure the vines to a wire wreath base.

HOW TO MAKE A TRADITIONAL BOW

MATERIALS

- 2½-yd. to 3-yd. (2.3 to 2.75 m) length of ribbon, 2" to 2½" (5 to 6.5 cm) wide.
- 22-gauge or 24-gauge floral wire; or chenille wire for bows that will be wired to packages or around woodwork.

1 Cut 18" (46 cm) length of ribbon; set aside for center tie. Starting 8" to 12" (20.5 to 30.5 cm) from end of remaining length of ribbon, fold 3½" to 4" (9 to 10 cm) loop with right side of ribbon facing out.

2 Fold a loop toward the opposite side, bringing ribbon underneath the tail to keep the right side of the ribbon facing out.

3 Continue wrapping the ribbon, making loops that fan slightly, until there are three or four loops on each side with a second tail extending.

4 Bend wire around ribbon at center; twist wire tightly, gathering ribbon. Hold wire firmly at the top, and turn the bow, twisting wire snug.

5 Fold width of 18" (46 cm) ribbon into thirds through the middle portion of ribbon. Tie ribbon around center of the bow, knotting it on the back of the bow.

6 Separate loops. Trim tails as desired.

HOW TO MAKE A CLUSTER BOW

MATERIALS

- Ribbon in desired width; calculate yardage as on page 5.
- 22-gauge or 24-gauge floral wire; or chenille wire for bows that will be wired to packages or around woodwork.

1 Place thumb and index finger at determined length for tail, with ribbon right side up. Fold the ribbon back on itself at a diagonal, with wrong sides together, so ribbon forms a right angle.

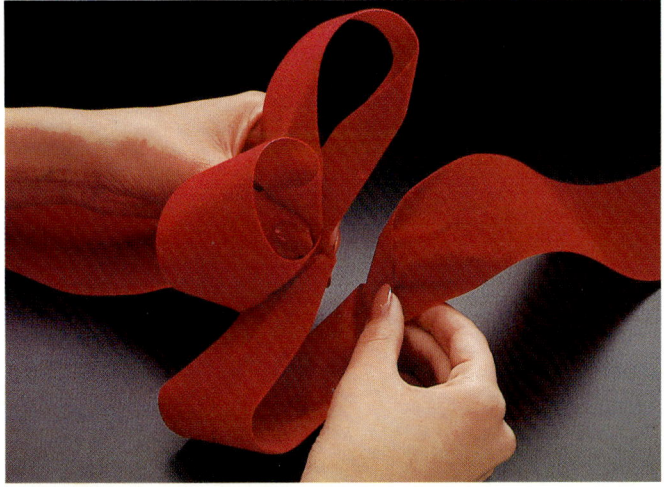

2 Wrap ribbon over thumb to form center loop; secure with fingers. Twist ribbon one-half turn at underside of loop, so the right side of the ribbon faces up.

3 Form first loop. Twist ribbon one-half turn, and form loop on opposite side.

4 Continue forming loops under the previous loops, alternating sides and twisting ribbon so right side always faces up; make each loop slightly larger than the loop above it.

5 When final loop has been formed, insert wire through center of bow. Bend wire around ribbon at center; twist wire tightly, gathering ribbon. Hold wire firmly at the top and turn the bow, twisting wire snug. Separate and shape the loops.

WREATHS

Nothing echoes a Christmas tradition more than wreaths. You can make your own from fresh, preserved, or artificial greens. Or purchase ready-made wreaths and add your own embellishments. Fresh evergreen and eucalyptus wreaths, both easy to make, add fragrance to a room. Other wreath styles, including grapevine and twig wreaths, are available at craft and floral stores.

You may choose to embellish an entire wreath, use a third of the wreath as the design area, or add a single embellishment. It is usually more attractive if the focal point of the design is slightly offset.

Choose embellishments that are in scale with the size of the wreath, and vary the size of the embellishments so there will be a dominant focal point, with smaller items that complement it. Choose items that are harmonious in style, yet provide some contrast in color and texture. Several suggestions for embellishing wreaths are shown on pages 11 to 14.

HOW TO MAKE A FRESH EVERGREEN WREATH

MATERIALS

- Fresh greens.
- 22-gauge or 24-gauge paddle floral wire; wire cutter; pruning shears.
- Coat hanger.
- Ribbon and embellishments as desired.

1 Shape coat hanger into circle. Cut greens into sprigs. Wire three sprigs to hanger, with tips facing up, placing two in front and one in back; wrap wire at base of sprigs.

2 Continue wrapping clusters of greens with wire, overlapping each cluster to conceal wire. When coat hanger is covered, cut some full tips of greens and wire them to hanger, concealing ends of sprigs.

HOW TO MAKE A EUCALYPTUS WREATH

MATERIALS

- Ready-made straw wreath.
- Eucalyptus with fine stems; two or three bunches will be sufficient for most wreath sizes.
- 22-gauge or 24-gauge paddle floral wire; wire cutter; pruning shears.
- Ribbon and embellishments as desired.

1 Cut eucalyptus in half or in thirds, so each sprig is 6" to 7" (15 to 18 cm) long. Secure the bottom 1" (2.5 cm) of several sprigs to wreath with wire, wrapping the wire around wreath; cover front and sides of wreath.

2 Continue adding sprigs to front and sides of wreath; layer sprigs and wrap with wire, working in one direction. Stagger the length of the tips randomly.

3 Lift tips of sprigs at starting point, and secure last layer of sprigs under them. Make a wire loop for hanging; secure loop to back of the wreath. Embellish as desired.

TIPS FOR EMBELLISHING WREATHS

Secure ribbon tails with hot glue, arranging twists and loops.

Make picks by grouping items together. Attach wire to items as necessary. Wrap stems and wires with floral tape.

Separate bunches of dried flowers by holding them over steam for 1 to 2 minutes; remove from steam and pull stems apart gently.

Attach wire to pinecone by wrapping wire around bottom layers of pinecone.

Add wire as necessary to fragile stems of dried flowers, to strengthen them. Wrap stem and wire with floral tape.

Attach wire to cinnamon stick by inserting it through the length of the stick; wrap the wire around the stick, twisting ends at middle. Trim wire, leaving 6" (15 cm) ends for attaching to wreath.

Create a base for anchoring embellishments by wiring a piece of floral foam, which has been covered with moss, to the wreath. Attach embellishments to moss-covered base.

Shape an artificial wreath made on a single wire into a candy cane or swag. Cut the wreath apart where the wire was joined.

Add luster to pinecones by applying glossy brown aerosol paint.

Spray artificial snow on wreath for a lightly flocked appearance.

Highlight twigs and vines with frost or glitter aerosol paint.

Keep a balanced look when embellishing an entire wreath by dividing wreath into three or four sections; distribute items evenly within each section.

Display wreath over a length of wide ribbon for added color. Embellish the top of the ribbon with a sprig.

MORE IDEAS FOR WREATHS

Snowman ornaments add a whimsical touch to this artificial wreath. The light misting of artificial snow, the tiny purchased sleds, and the candy canes carry out the wintery holiday theme.

Victorian wreath made from eucalyptus (page 10) features a pearlescent cherub on a pastel satin bow. Statice and clustered pastel embellishments are used throughout the wreath.

Musical theme on this fresh evergreen wreath (page 10) was created using purchased instrument ornaments and paper fans made from sheet music.

Dried naturals are the primary embellishments for this ready-made twig wreath. The bird's nest, slightly off-center on the wreath, becomes the focal point.

Silver and gold are combined for this wreath. Silver aerosol paint is used to highlight the greens, and a sheer silver ribbon becomes a strong focal point. Touches of gold are introduced in the smaller embellishments.

Evergreen bouquet of mixed greens and pinecones is wired asymmetrically onto a ready-made grapevine wreath for a quick embellishment. The narrow French ribbon is wrapped loosely around the wreath.

Gold and red metallics are used for a dramatic effect, and the embellishments are offset for even more impact. The ready-made straw wreath used as the base was concealed with metallic ribbon and tiny garland.

Apples and popcorn are used as the dominant embellishments for this fresh wreath of mixed greens (page 10). To carry out the natural look, nuts and pinecones are also used.

Add the true look of Christmas to your home with <u>Holiday Wreaths, Garlands & Bows</u>. *Full-color photos show you how to quickly and easily make them all!*

Nothing shouts "Christmas!" as much as beautiful wreaths, garlands and bows throughout your home. These seasonal decorations cheerfully greet you and your guests at your door, add spice to all your rooms, halls and stairways, and just seem to radiate the season's good feelings! Now you can affordably create your own decorations, with the full-color, instructional photographs in *Holiday Wreaths, Garlands & Bows* guiding you. Inside, you'll discover how to:

- Put together beautiful wreaths — using traditional evergreens and intriguing "new" materials

- Make a variety of graceful garlands

- Create luxurious holiday bows that will add extra color to decorations, help you wrap packages with class, and more

Now you don't have to spend a fortune at the store to decorate with traditional wreaths, garlands and bows. This photo-filled book shows you how to easily make them all, start to finish. Plus — your results will be beautiful and economical!

ISBN-0-86573-917-X

0 52944 08106 5